GO FACTS FOOD

Cooking and Change

Cooking and Change

© Blake Publishing 2003
Additional material © A & C Black Publishers Ltd 2005

First published 2003 in Australia by Blake Education Pty Ltd

This edition published 2005 in the United Kingdom by
A & C Black Publishers Ltd, 37 Soho Square, London W1D 3QZ
www.acblack.com

ISBN-10: 0-7136-7287-0
ISBN-13: 978-0-7136-7287-9

A CIP record for this book is available from the British Library.

Written by Paul McEvoy
Design and layout by The Modern Art Production Group
Photos by Paul McEvoy, John Foxx, Photodisc, Brand X, Corbis,
Digital Stock, Eyewire and Artville.

UK series consultant: Julie Garnett

Printed in China by WKT Company Ltd.

A & C Black uses paper produced with elemental chlorine-free pulp,
harvested from managed sustainable forests.

Cooking Changes Food

Food changes when it is frozen, chilled, heated or mixed with other foods.

You can prepare or cook food in many ways. Each cooking method gives food a different taste, look or **texture**. Cooking makes food more interesting and tasty.

Recipes are directions that tell cooks what **ingredients** to use. They also tell how much of each ingredient is needed. Recipes describe how to put the ingredients together and how long to cook the food.

Every country has its own cooking style.

5

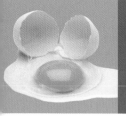

Cooking and Heat

Cooking changes the way food tastes and feels. It can also kill germs that make people sick.

We use heat to cook food. Foods can be fried, boiled, grilled, steamed and baked using heat.

The texture of food changes when it is cooked. Raw eggs are a gooey liquid. After being cooked, eggs become a soft, warm solid. In a toaster, soft bread becomes dry, crunchy toast. Some foods, such as meat and vegetables, are cooked to make them easier to chew.

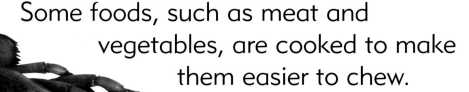

Vegetables like courgettes, broccoli, carrots and beans become tender and soft when cooked.

Toasted bread is easier to spread with butter and jam.

Eggs can be fried, poached or scrambled for breakfast.

Popcorn Recipe

Popcorn seeds must be heated and popped to be eaten.

Each popcorn seed has a small amount of water inside its hard shell. When the seed is heated, the water **expands** and the shell pops.

How to Make Popcorn

Ask an adult for help when you cook. Use a pot holder when the pan is hot.

You will need:

- $\frac{1}{2}$ cup of popping corn
- 2 tablespoons of vegetable oil
- a pot with a lid
- a pot holder

1 Put the oil into the pot. Add the popping corn.

2 Cover the pot with a lid. Place the pot on the stove. Set the stove to medium heat.

3 Don't open the lid while the corn is popping. Gently move the pot over the burner. Turn off the heat when the popping stops.

4 Pour the popcorn into a large bowl. Let it cool down before you eat it.

Cooking Mixtures

Breads, cakes and biscuits are all made from a mixture of flour and other ingredients. The mixture is then cooked in an oven.

Bread is made from a **mixture** of flour, **yeast**, water and other flavouring ingredients. Wheat flour and yeast are needed to make breads that will **rise**. Flat breads are made without yeast.

Cakes, muffins and biscuits are made by mixing sugar, eggs and sometimes milk or butter with the flour. The thick, wet **batter** is then poured into tins and cooked in the oven.

Special cooking tools, like scrapers, whisks and mixers, help people cook batters and mixes.

Most mixes contain flour made of wheat, corn, oats or rice.

11

Pancake Recipe

Dry and wet ingredients are mixed together to make pancake batter.

The liquid batter becomes a bread-like pancake after it is cooked. Some people enjoy eating pancakes with maple syrup or with fruit.

How to make 12 small pancakes
You will need:

- 1 egg
- 1 cup of milk
- $1\frac{1}{2}$ cups of flour
- 3 tablespoons of sugar
- a pinch of salt
- butter or oil
- a non-stick frying pan, two bowls and a whisk

1 In a small bowl, beat the egg with a whisk and add the milk. Place the flour, sugar and salt in a large bowl.

2 Slowly pour the milk mixture into the flour. Keep stirring all the time until you have a smooth batter.

3 Heat a teaspoon of butter or oil in the frying pan. Add 1 large spoonful of batter to the pan.

4 Cook over medium heat until the bubbles pop. Flip the pancake over and cook on the other side until golden brown.

Cold and Frozen Foods

When food is kept cold it stays fresher. Other foods are eaten frozen, such as ice-cream and ice lollies.

Refrigerated foods stay fresh longer. Food left in a warm place will **rot** quickly. **Frozen** foods can stay fresh and good to eat for months.

Some food is eaten frozen which changes its taste and texture. Ice-cream is a frozen mixture of milk, cream, sugar and flavours. Ice lollies are a frozen mixture of water or juice with sugar and other flavours.

How many foods can you think of that are refrigerated or frozen?

15

Ice Lolly Recipe

Frozen fruit juices make delicious ice lollies.

Liquids become icy solids when they are frozen.

How to make 4 to 6 ice lollies.

You will need:

- 1 cup of your favourite juice
- 6 strawberries or a banana (You can also try an orange, raspberries, a pear or a peach.)
- ice lolly tray

1 Chop the strawberries or banana into small pieces.

2 Place some chopped fruit into each part of the tray.

3 Fill with juice and add sticks.

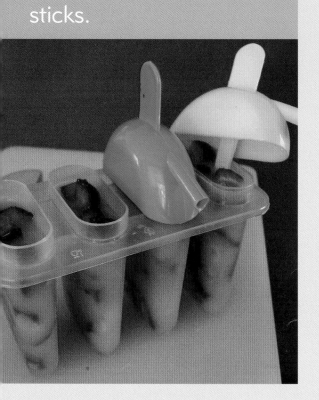

4 Freeze until solid.

17

How can cooking change food?

Raw	Mixed	Cooked

18

Glossary

batter   a mixture of flour, eggs and liquid

expand   grow in size

frozen   hardened by cold temperatures

ingredient   one part of a mixture

mixture   a combination of different things

rise   swell or puff up

rot   decay or go off

texture   the way something feels

yeast   something added to dough to make bread rise

Index